We Love EASTER

Saviour Pirotta

WAYLAND

Editor: Kirsty Hamilton
Senior Design Manager: Rosamund Saunders
Designer: Elaine Wilkinson

Published in Great Britain in 2006 by Wayland,
an imprint of Hachette Children's Books

The right of Saviour Pirotta to be identified as the author of
the work has been asserted by him in the Copyright, Designs
and Patents Act 1988.

British Library Cataloguing in Publication Data
Pirotta, Saviour
We love Easter
1.Easter – Juvenile literature
I.Title
394.2'667

ISBN 10: 0 7502 4836 X
ISBN 13: 978 07502 4836 5

Printed in China

Wayland
An imprint of Hachette Children's Books
338 Euston Road, London NW1 3BH

The publishers would like to thank the following for
allowing us to reproduce their pictures in this book:

Corbis: title page, 9, Ariel Skelley; 6, Albright-Knox Art
Gallery; 7, Richard T. Nowitz; 8, Lucidio Studio Inc.; 11,
Philip Gould; 12, Oswaldo Rivas; 15, Alinari Archives; 16,
Clay Perry; 18 Craig Aurness; cover, 23, Ronnie Kaufman /
Alamy: 17, Oote Boe; 20, PhotoCuisine. / Robert Harding:
4, 13, 14, 22 / Getty Images: 19, Jutta Klee, Taxi; 21, Paul
Webster, Stone / Wayland picture library: 5, 10

Contents

Easter is here!

Happy Easter! Happy Easter! All over the world, many people celebrate Easter. For Christians it is the biggest festival of the year.

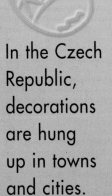

In the Czech Republic, decorations are hung up in towns and cities.

4

In some
countries,
children make
Easter cards to
send to friends
and family.

Easter can take place on
any Sunday between
the 22nd of March
and the 25th of
April. However,
Christians start
preparing for
it long before.

5

Artists such as Gauguin have painted Jesus's death on the cross.

Jesus is alive!

Easter is the happy ending to a sad story. Although the Christian leader **Jesus Christ** taught people how to love one another and God, he was put to death by men who did not understand him.

DID YOU KNOW?

Jesus lived 2000 years ago. He was born in a village called Nazareth, in the country of Palestine.

But Christians believe Jesus came back to life three days later.

When Jesus's friends visited his tomb, they found it empty. The tomb can still be seen in Israel today.

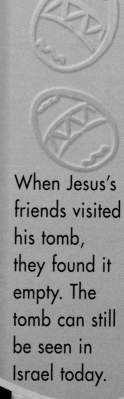

New life

In countries of the northern **hemisphere**, Easter is in spring. Spring is the time when the earth also comes back to life after the cold, dark days of winter.

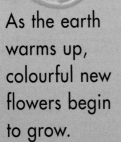

As the earth warms up, colourful new flowers begin to grow.

New leaves appear on the trees. Plants and flowers grow again. What a lovely time to celebrate the new life of Jesus.

New-born lambs bring new life at Easter.

Preparing for Easter

Some people make **pancakes** the day before Lent.

Christians start to prepare for Easter forty days before. This is a period called **Lent**. It starts on a special day called Ash Wednesday.

DID YOU KNOW?

People have their foreheads marked with ash to show they are sorry for their wrongdoings.

During Lent many people give up treats, like sweets or watching their favourite television programme, to show Jesus they are grateful for what he did.

In the Caribbean, people have a carnival before Lent. They wear colourful costumes.

Holy Week

The last week of Lent is called Holy Week. It begins on Palm Sunday, a day when people welcomed Jesus as their king and laid **palm** branches at his feet.

In some churches, people are given a small cross, made of palm fronds.

In many places, Christians carry palm branches and join the Palm Sunday **procession** in which a **statue** of Jesus is carried.

In parts of Africa, people carry decorated crosses through the streets.

13

Good Friday

On Good Friday, many church bells are kept silent in honour of Jesus.

Jesus died on the Friday before Easter, a day Christians call Good Friday. Good Friday is a very **solemn** day. Many churches are draped in black cloth, and there may be processions showing scenes of the last few hours of Jesus's life.

DID YOU KNOW?

In church, the Good Friday service is based on the things Jesus said before he died on the cross.

This painting shows how Jesus shared bread and wine with his friends the day before he died.

Happy Easter!

The serious mood of Good Friday lasts until Saturday night, when Christians spend time thinking about what Jesus means to them. Then Easter Sunday is a happy day.

On Easter Sunday flowers fill the church with perfume.

DID YOU KNOW?

Many countries have a procession to celebrate Jesus's return.

Church bells ring to announce that Jesus has come back to life. Churches are filled with flowers.

People go to mass on Easter Sunday and light candles to celebrate.

17

Delicious eggs

Many children are given a chocolate egg for Easter. The egg is a symbol of Easter because a chick, a new life, comes out of it when it hatches. In the past, eggs were used to celebrate Spring.

In the Ukraine, Easter eggs are decorated with beautiful patterns and colours.

Hunting for
Easter eggs
is a popular
game.

Today, people in
Eastern Europe
still decorate
real eggs with
beautiful
patterns.

19

Time for a feast

Lamb, the symbol of Jesus, is the most popular Easter meal in many countries.

After giving up treats in Lent, people like to enjoy good food at Easter.

Easter treats vary around the world. Cypriots have a special Easter cheesecake. Italians tuck into a cake shaped like a dove, called a colomba.

In England, hot cross buns are enjoyed at Easter.

21

Let's celebrate!

Mexican Indians perform a traditional Easter dance.

In Mexico people take to the streets to eat and drink. In France, children are told to watch out for flying church bells while their parents hide eggs in the garden for them to find.

There are also **pageants** in the streets.
Everyone is glad that Jesus is risen.
Happy Easter! Happy Easter!

School children in Britain make Easter bonnets and dress up for an Easter parade.

23

Index and glossary

Ash the powder that is left when something has been burnt
Jesus Christ the person who started the Christian religion
Lent the forty days before Easter, when Christians give up treats
Nazareth the place where Jesus Christ was born
hemisphere one half of the planet Earth, divided by a line called the equator
pageant a colourful parade
palm a tropical tree with fan-shaped leaves
pancake a thin flat cake made from flour, egg and milk
procession a group of people moving forward together
solemn when a person or event is serious
statue a crafted figure of a person or animal